RUSSIAN STYLE

Text © Evelina Khromtchenko
© 2009 Assouline Publishing

Assouline Publishing
601 West 26th Street
18th floor
New York, NY 10001
USA
Tel.: 212 989-6810   Fax: 212 647-0005
www.assouline.com

ISBN: 9782 75940 3950
All rights reserved.

Color separation by Luc Alexis Chasleries
Printed in Singapore

EVELINA KHROMTCHENKO

RUSSIAN
STYLE

ASSOULINE

FOREWORD

Three years ago Kelly Killoren Bensimon came to me with an idea for a fashion-inspired book titled *American Style.* With an unusual perspective of historical and iconic images, Kelly explored American fashion through social history, designers, and select celebrities and personalities who influenced the way Americans dress today. The book was a great success that has provided insight into what defines style in this country, since the early 19th century.

So when we met Evelina Khromtchenko, who was so enthusiastic about the evolution and history of her country, we couldn't wait to get started on a book on Russian style. We thought that an effective way to illustrate such a rich, complex, largely unknown, and extremely influential region of the world would be to explore icons that have come to define this country. Then we decided to open the subject to general culture. The idea was to illuminate Russia's DNA in all its aspects, but always with an art and fashion angle. In this book we have aimed to represent the most remarkable symbols of the country's past, and also the new national figures and concepts that define its contemporary culture.

Here are the results—your A to Z guide to understanding the mystery of Russian style!

MARTINE ASSOULINE

(Left page) Tatlin tower, image by Serge Lutens, 1989

To my great country, where I am happy to have been born,

and to my son, whose generation will write new, exciting chapters.

INTRODUCTION

In every country and in every culture, there are stereotypes that form a prism through which a society and its inhabitants are perceived internationally. *Russian Style* is the visual narrative of the stereotypes that have come to define our national identity, as well as the lesser-known places, people, crafts, and ideas that are rooted in more than eleven centuries of Russian history.

In 1990, the Soviet way of life, which seemed solid and well meaning to those living inside the country, was blasted around the world. A "wind of change" swept the country. I was a teenager at the time, but I understood that there was something to be saved among the ruins of our empire.

During the post-perestroika years, when I would visit Europe and the United States, people would ask me where I was from. When I said, "I am Russian," their responses were usually, "Caviar, vodka, *matryoshka*, ballet, Malevich, Dostoyevsky, Ded Moroz, '*Za Zdorovie!*'" I was pleased by their attempts to connect with some of the more common themes of my culture, but I wanted the world to know more. In 2003 we decided to devote the fiftieth anniversary issue of *L'Officiel* Russia, of which I am the editor in chief, to the theme "Made in Russia." We started with a list of the Western world's distinct stereotypes of Russia. The list appeared enormous, especially in comparison with those of other countries. Then I came up with my own formula, which I present in this book. For me, Russian style is not only *rubashka* and high boots, furs and brocade, Vologda laces and *kokoshnik,* but it is also the mysterious Russian soul, and a way of living with a belief in miracles. It is a man's might and a woman's beauty.

It is great accomplishments in literature, from Pushkin's fairy tales to Tolstoy's *Anna Karenina*, and remarkable art—both old masterpieces stored at historic national museums and the contemporary works of young Russian artists featured in trendy urban galleries. Deep snow, the effect of sunlight on golden domes, splendid Saint Petersburg, cozy Moscow . . . the things we have, and the things we have lost.

This book is created in the form of an engaging encyclopedia. Many of the items I chose to illustrate are specifically connected to the world of fashion. When deciding on these entries, I was helped by some of the best minds in the fashion business, who for many years have been providing me with thoughtful answers to the question: "What comes to your mind when you hear the word 'Russia'?"

It was important to me to impart to readers that nowadays Russia is becoming more and more relevant in the world of fashion. Magazines, ads, and catwalks are filled with Russian models, the most famous of whom is Natalia Vodianova. Russians are desirable clients at fashion boutiques in the most important capitals of the world. Top designers create collections inspired by Russia, and magazines produce fashion shoots in the Russian style, which is usually translated as one of the following: The richly decorated aristocratic costumes found in fairy tales and paintings that predate the reforms of Peter the Great; the Russified Western dress under Catherine the Great; colorful Russian folk clothes; images of the mysterious princess Anastasia; the post-revolution designs and work uniforms of Varvara Stepanova; classical ballet costumes inspired by the images of magical swans created by Anna Pavlova and Maya Plisetskaya; and Soviet symbols like the red star and army uniform, portrayed in Elton John's music video "Nikita."

What most of these components of Russian style have in common is that they each emerged alongside dramatic political reforms. Peter the Great, after instituting sweeping changes to the military and church, ordered all men to westernize their dress and shave their beards and mustaches; he instructed boyars, or noblemen, to permit their wives and daughters to wear their hair uncovered, a practice traditionally considered highly indecent. Russian women were encouraged to adopt the plunging neckline, which was viewed as audacious for according to the Orthodox Church, the holy cross had to be hidden under one's clothes. (As a result of Peter's reform, the chains on which the crosses were worn were lengthened, a style evident in eighteenth-century Russian portraits.)

But Peter's dress code would be Russified just a few decades later by a German-born woman—the fifteen-year-old princess Sophia Augusta Frederica. She had been secretly brought to Moscow by her ambitious mother, christened as Catherine, married to Peter III in 1745, and crowned empress in 1762. Catherine the Great brought back elements of traditional Russian clothing, including dresses with convertible sleeves and a small *kokoshnik* worn with veils. She developed a court uniform that would be maintained by Russia's imperial dynasties, replications of which can be seen in Anatole Litvak's film *Anastasia* (1956).

Though Russian royal families are popularly envisioned as regally dressed and living in ornate surroundings with servants at their beck and call, this image is often fictitious. Her Imperial Highness the Grand Duchess Anastasia Nikolaevna Romanova, Emperor Nicholas II's youngest daughter, shared her room with her sister Maria, slept on a narrow soldier's bench, and was allowed no other luxury than a couple of drops of violet-scented Coty perfume in her warm evening bath. The morning bath was cold, and the girls had to carry the water for themselves, without the assistance of servants. Legend has it that in 1918, on what is considered to have been her seventeenth birthday, shortly before the czar's entire family was shot by a Bolshevik firing squad, Anastasia was learning how to bake bread.

In spite of the simplicity characteristic of the Russian aristocracy of the early twentieth century, today "Russian" in many circles has become an adjective connoting luxury. The reason is not only the fantastic jeweled costumes of the period before Peter the Great's reforms, when richness of dress was extremely important. The fantasy of the "Eastern fairy tale" was integrated into the definition of Russian style by artistic forces such as Sergei Diaghilev's Ballets Russes, known as much for its mysterious sets and costumes created by Léon Bakst as for its dancing. Bakst's sketches for the theater have become the prototype for fashion illustrators; he himself worked for the houses of Paul Poiret and Jeanne Paquin, illustrated magazines, and came close to opening his own fashion house. The great artist was not afraid of engaging with the fashion world.

The passion for simplicity came back into international fashion with the Great Depression and, in Russia, the revolution of 1917. The revolution gave birth to a burst of avant-garde experiments in art and fashion. In Old Russian, the same word is used for both "red" and "beautiful." Vladimir Lenin brought red back into fashion, adding an ideological meaning, while avant-garde artists strengthened the color's impact by building a new visual world around it.

While the artists were making *Prozodezhda*, or red stars, and inventing new fabric prints, the couturiers, whose clients had all fled, were dressing new customers. Nadezhda Lamanova, the legendary designer to the czars, lost all she had, but she did not emigrate, as she couldn't imagine a life for herself outside Russia. Her right to vote was revoked because she had worked for the royal family, and even though she had begun to create clothes for the Soviet leaders' wives, she was imprisoned. In the 1920s, together with a group of artists including Vera Mukhina and Alexandra Exter, Lamanova continued with her immaculate handiwork and traditional Russian sewing techniques, but by then her aim was to invent a comfortable, everyday national uniform based on the country's new ideals. In 1925, during the Exposition Internationale des Arts Décoratifs et Industriels Modernes in Paris, her works won a grand prize. Nevertheless, according to legend, in the autumn of 1941 the eighty-year-old Lamanova told her friend Mukhina, "You know, I will die soon. I have only two drops of Coty left."

At the turn of the millennium, a new Russian generation was born. For us, The Soviet Union is not a monster, but the happy country of our childhoods, one in which you didn't have to think about where the candies came from or why you had to wear a red tie. This was the country where our favorite dolls and teddy bears lived, where delicious *pirozhki* were baked, where the cartoons were exciting and the songs merry, and where your mama was the most beautiful woman in the world.

Making money, traveling all over the world, rushing to try everything that life offers, and launching our own brand of "luxury," we are now realizing that we have forgotten some of the most essential tokens of our childhoods and national traditions, along with our country's heritage. This book presents those memories, as well as the symbols of contemporary Russia that will define and drive our future.

Boyars, ballet dancers, and the grand duchess Anastasia will stay with us. Our national identity, childhood happiness, and the characteristics of Russia today all come together to make up Russian style. So, *dobro pozhalovat'*! Enjoy!

EVELINA KHROMTCHENKO

R

RUSSIAN FASHION WEEK

Russia's biggest fashion event, produced by Alexander Shumsky (third from left), has promoted a new wave of talent, including Dmitry Loginov, Vassa, Julia Dalakian, Max Chernitsov, and Olga Romina. Every April and October, RFW presents more than 60 collections from Russia and the former Soviet republics. International fashion brands also take part to introduce themselves to the Russian market.

A
AVANT-GARDE

Architect Vladimir Tatlin's eponymous tower, artists Kazimir Malevich and El Lissitzky's geometric paintings, photographer Alexander Rodchenko's daring angles, and the fashion designs of Varvara Stepanova were all part of this early-20th-century movement of Russian artists who shared the dream of reconstructing the environment via the creation of the logical and efficient. The Russian avant-garde has inspired many designers, including John Galliano, who created this dress for Dior Haute Couture.

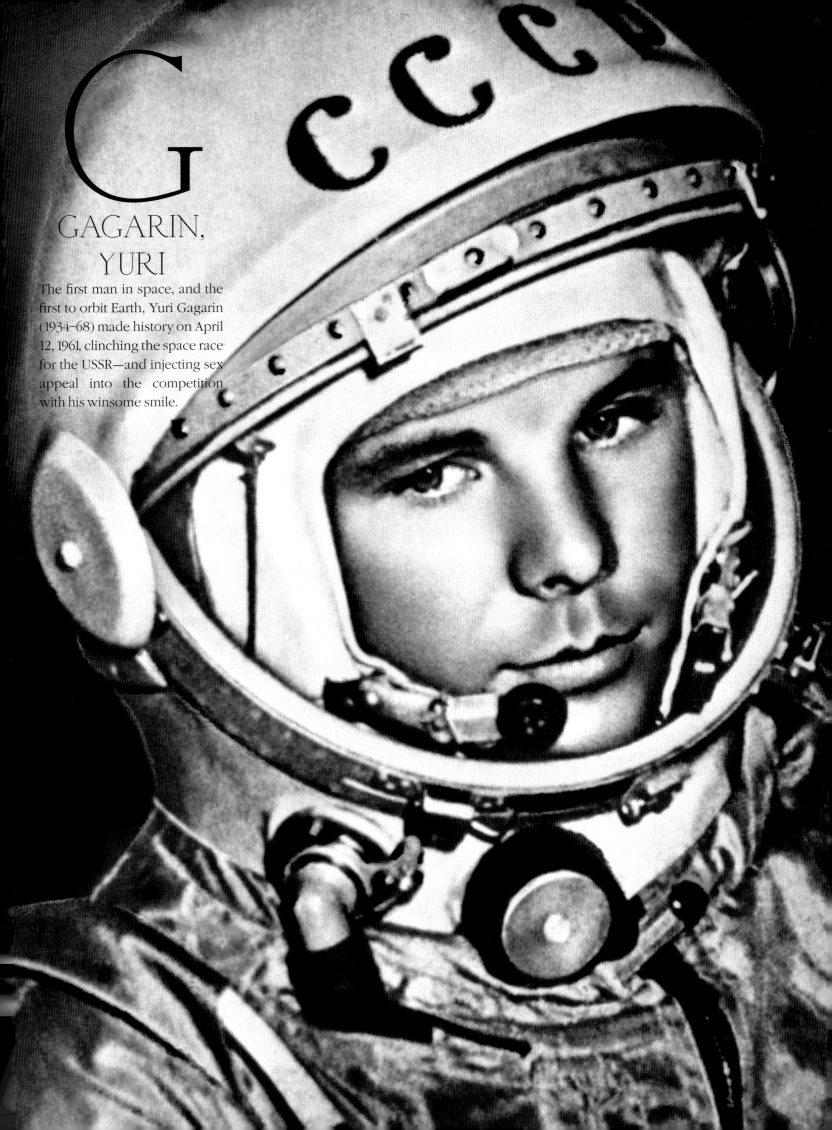

G

GAGARIN, YURI

The first man in space, and the first to orbit Earth, Yuri Gagarin (1934–68) made history on April 12, 1961, clinching the space race for the USSR—and injecting sex appeal into the competition with his winsome smile.

Z
ZVEZDA

In China, the pentagram embodies the union of five elements; in Christian culture, it stands for Jesus Christ's five wounds; and in Soviet Russia, the five points were said to represent the social groups that would lead to Communism—youth, the military, industrial laborers, agricultural workers, and the intelligentsia. The red star eventually came to represent Communism and Socialism.

N
NINA DONIS

Nina Donis, designed by Nina Neretina and Donis Poupis, was the first Russian fashion brand to win a prize at France's Hyères fashion festival. Inspired by Yuri Gagarin, their design aesthetic is based on constructivism.

K

KIRILLITZA

In 863, Cyril developed a precursor to the Russian alphabet based on Greek with the help of his brother Methodius. Dating to the 10th century, Cyrillic characters are used in many Eastern European languages and can be considered a metaphor for the cryptic Russian psyche.

B

BESKOZIRKA

The *beskozirka*, or sailor's cap, became part of the Russian naval uniform in 1811, followed by the *telnyashka*, or striped sailor's shirt, in 1874. Together they have come to symbolize the revolution, which began aboard the cruiser ship *Aurora*. The peakless hat was adopted into the naval uniform of many countries.

S
SHITYE

This ornate, gold embroidery craft came to Russia in the 10th century, when the country was joining the Christian faith. Encrusted with pearls and gems and sewn with gold thread, *shitye* garments were originally used in religious rituals and later became popular with the imperial family and nobility.

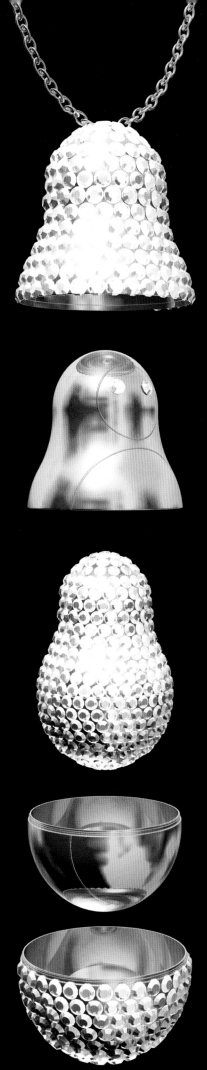

M
MATRYOSHKA

The *matryoshka* has come to serve as a metaphor for the complexity and multifarious layers of the Russian woman. The first wooden nesting doll, which consisted of 33 heroes from Pushkin's fairy tales, was carved in the 1890s by artist Sergei Malyutin and inspired by the statue of Fukorokuju, the Japanese god of wisdom.

S

SIMATCHËV, DENIS

What started in 2002 with a T-shirt featuring a portrait of Vladimir Putin framed in floral embroidery has evolved into a fashion brand based on evocative visual symbols of the Soviet era, including "propaganda" cartoons and traditional Russian folk art, such as Khokhloma.

A
AKHMATOVA, ANNA

Anna Andreevna Gorenko (1889–1966), who took the pen name Anna Akhmatova, was one of the first great female Russian poets, along with her competitor, Marina Tsvetaeva. Her profile, short bangs, and iconic look—slim, sad-eyed, and dressed in fringed shawls—inspired many artists, including Amedeo Modigliani.

S

STEPANOVA, VARVARA

In 1923 Alexander Rodchenko's wife, the painter and designer Varvara Stepanova (1894–1958), published the Prozodezhda Manifesto, declaring that the main principles of clothing design should be comfort, simplicity, and practicality. She created unisex uniforms for workers from surgeons to firefighters; her innovative designs used simple geometric forms and industrial themes rather than floral and folkloric patterns.

B
BALLERINA

Russian ballerinas—Anna Pavlova, Tamara Karsavina, Galina Ulanova, and Maya Plisetskaya (pictured), to name a few—are practically viewed as goddesses. What is their secret? Says Plisetskaya, "It is important to dance the music, not to music . . ."

Z

ZHOSTOVO

This village outside Moscow has been famous for its traditional hand-painted steel trays with ornate flowers since the 19th century.

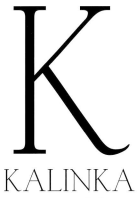

K
KALINKA

The best-known Russian folk song of all time is actually not a folk song—it was composed by Ivan Petrovitch Larionov in 1860 for a theatrical production. Its legendary melody has been selected as the theme song for everything from films to video games.

G

GORKY PARK

Gorky Park, a crime novel by Martin Cruz Smith published in 1981, takes its name from this famous Moscow amusement park. Because the controversial novel predated glasnost, the 1983 movie version was filmed in Finland. "I follow the Moskva/ Down to Gorky Park/ Listening to the wind of change..." sang the Scorpions in 1990.

B

BOY BABA

In Russian, *boy baba* translates as "female warrior." The expression refers to the stereotypical Russian feminist or free-thinking woman, for which Alexandra Kollontaï (1872–1952), a Communist leader known for her radical theories on love and marriage, and the first woman to serve in the Soviet government, is the paradigm.

P
PUGACHEVA, ALLA

Referred to as "the prima donna," Russia's most popular musical performer launched her career in the 1960s and became a style icon for generations of Soviet and post-Soviet women. Pugacheva has put her name on everything from perfume and potato chips to footwear.

R
RED SQUARE

Moscow's central square, site of Saint Basil's Cathedral, Lenin's Tomb, and the Historical Museum, is the country's principal symbol of national identity. It takes its name not only from the adjacent Kremlin's red bricks, but also from the old Russian word for "red," which can also mean "beautiful."

H

HLEB

When you say *hleb*, or "bread," in Russia, you are most certainly talking about rye bread, as it is the most popular kind. Legend has it that Christianity divided into the Orthodox and Roman Catholic churches in 1054 partly because the West was using unleavened bread and Russians didn't want to let go of their traditional rye.

C

CHAIKA

Social hierarchies in Soviet Russia were so well defined that you could guess who was inside a car based on its make. The Chaika was the car of Kremlin bosses, while military generals and government officials rode in chauffeured Volgas. The Zhiguli was favored by intellectuals and artists, and the more affordable Zaporozhet was driven by engineers, teachers, and doctors.

A

ALKOGOLICHKA

The Russian equivalent of the American "wife-beater," this sleeveless men's undershirt derives its name from the stereotype of the working-class male, who is imagined to be fond of drink.

S

"SHAIBU! SHAIBU!"

Shaiba means "puck," and *"Shaibu! Shaibu!"* is
what fans chant at Russian hockey games in hopes
of a goal. When the Soviet Union vied for the International Ice Hockey Federation's world cham-
pionship for the first time in 1954, its team won,
and the legend of Russian hockey—"the Big Red
Machine"—began. Many Russian players, such as
Pavel Bure (pictured), nicknamed "The Russian
Rocket," have played in the NHL.

P

PARAD

Moscow's Red Square is world renowned as the site of victory parades, rallies, and revolutions. The Russian word *mayka*, or T-shirt, was first introduced in 1938 to refer to a short-sleeved cotton sports top, which some say originated from the May Day parades.

T
TENNIS

"Only the ball should bounce." This ad slogan for an athletic bra emblazoned across Anna Kournikova's tennis shirt introduced sports fans around the world to Russia's female tennis stars, including Anastasia Myskina, Dinara Safina, and eventually Maria Sharapova (pictured), winner of Wimbledon and U.S. Open titles and spokeswoman for Tiffany, TAG Heuer, Nike, Canon, Land Rover, and Cole Haan.

I

IGMAND, ALEXANDER

In the 1970s designer Alexander Igmand (1942–2006), replaced the Soviet party's traditional caps with *shapkas,* supposedly in response to Leonid Brezhnev's complaints that his ears were freezing. A popular men's designer in the Soviet era, Igmand dressed Brezhnev (pictured) until the Soviet premier's death in 1982.

K
KON'KI

Skating is a national pastime, and Russian figure skaters such as Evgeni Plushenko (pictured in 2005), are renown for excelling in international competitions. Each year a skating rink is erected in Red Square in front of GUM. The Russian word for "skates" is *kon'ki*, or "little horses," as the blades were traditionally each shaped like the head of a stallion.

M
MUZIKA

Tchaikovsky, Rimsky-Korsakov, Mussorgsky, Glinka, Rachmaninoff, Stravinsky, Prokofiev, Shostakovich, Richter, Oistrakh, Rostropovich . . . Russian music is legendary, and its world-renowned maestros can be identified by their extreme intensity and expressiveness.

C

CHAPURIN, IGOR

One of Russia's best-known designers, Chapurin shows his collection during Paris Fashion Week. Whitney Houston, Pink, Cher, Beyoncé, Natalia Vodianova, and Miss Universe contestants have all worn his dresses, and the Chapurin store on Moscow's posh Kuznetskiy Most attracts the city's most fashionable denizens.

S

SIBIR

This mysterious, remote, and frigid land, rich in natural resources, stretches across the country, from the Ural Mountains to the Far East. Prisoners and dissenters were exiled here in both czarist and Stalinist times. The natives are known to wear clothes that are both colorful and unusual.

G
GIMNASTKI

Alina Kabaeva (pictured), Larisa Latynina, Svetlana Khorkina, Olga Korbut . . . Russian gymnasts stun the world with their highly challenging routines and winning scores. They are renowned for their prowess—and beauty.

K
KHOKHLOMA

A traditional Russian wood-painting craft that dates back to the 17th century and features lacquered tableware and furniture in red, black, and gold natural patterns. The contemporary Moscow designer Denis Simachëv designed a helicopter, motorcycle, and surfboard in this classic style.

B
BELKA & STRELKA

These little dogs were the first creatures to spend a day in outer space, on the Soviet spaceship *Sputnik 5* in 1960. Strelka went on to have 6 puppies, one of which was presented to John F. Kennedy's daughter, Caroline, by Nikita Khrushchev. The cartoon movie *Star Dogs: Belka and Strelka* comes out in 2009.

V
VALENKI

Valenki are rustic-style boots made from felt and traditionally worn under galoshes. In 1997, *L'Officiel* Russia organized an exhibit of *valenki* modernized by Russian artists and designers at the Pushkin Museum of Fine Arts in Moscow.

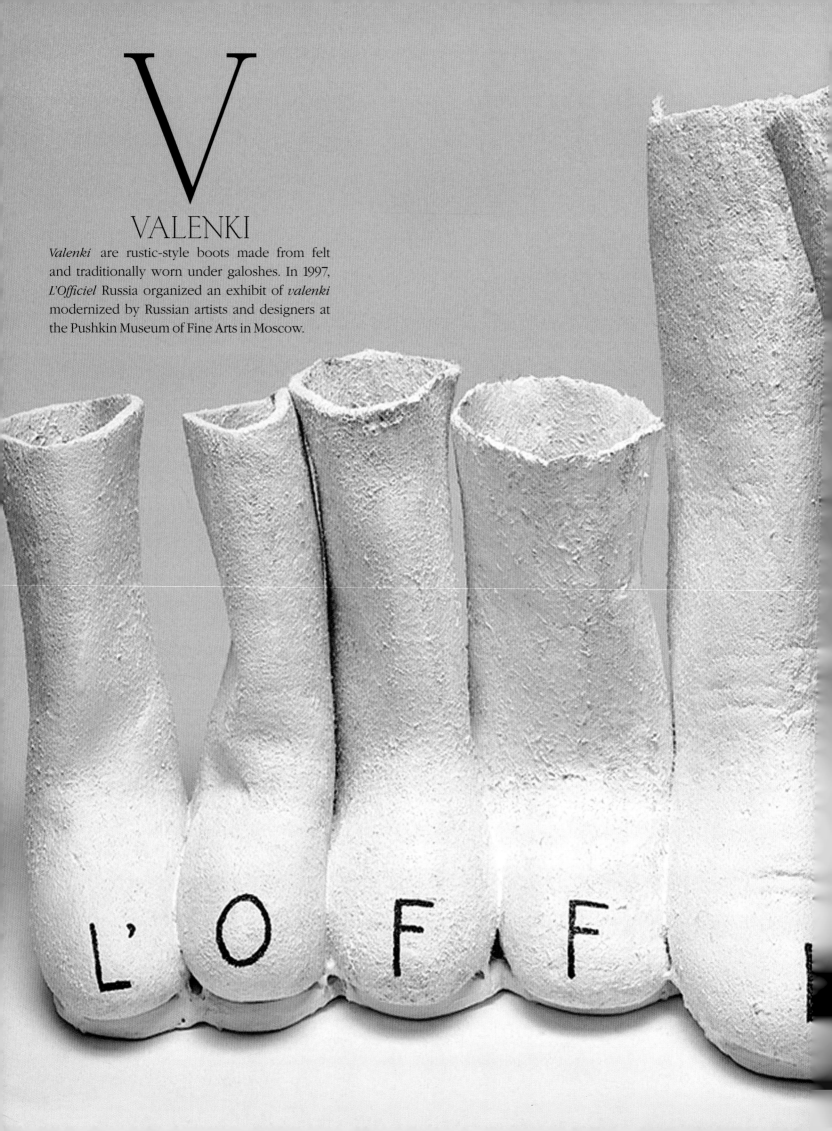

L

LAMANOVA, NADEZHDA

Couturier to the royal family and costume designer for the Moscow Art Theatre, Lamanova (1861–1941) opened her own atelier in Moscow in 1885 at age 24. After the fall of the czar in 1917, though she had the means to flee, Lamanova chose to stay in Russia and design for the new regime. She was held in high esteem by her contemporaries such as Paul Poiret and today her work is displayed in the Hermitage.

K

KRASAVITZA

Masha Kalinina, who won the Soviet Union's first beauty contest in 1988, traveled the world in pursuit of a career first as a model and then as a film star. She became a symbol of perestroika and started the wave of Russian models. *Krasavitza* is the Russian word for a beautiful woman.

L
LOSKUTKI

Loskutki, or Russian patchwork, is brightly colored and festive, and according to legend, originated in Gorodets, a city of craftspeople founded in 1152 by Yuri Dolgoruky. It is enjoying a revival on the runways of contemporary Russian designers.

P
PLATOK

Originally part of a Russian folk costume, the *platok,* a square piece of fabric, became the most popular head covering in the late 19th century. The fabric and color of a woman's *platok* gave insight into her age, class, and origin. In central Russia women knotted the *platok* under their chins, while in the north it was worn pinned up and called *ubrus*.

S
SAMOVAR

Much more than just a metal urn, the samovar evokes a whole lifestyle of hospitality. It is thought to have originated in Persia and today is a fixture in Russia and other Eastern and Middle Eastern countries. Tea leaves are stored in a pot at the top of the samovar and steeped with water boiled inside the urn.

S
STANISLAVSKY METHOD

Marilyn Monroe, Marlon Brando, Meryl Streep, and Robert De Niro were all influenced by the Stanislavsky method, an approach to acting developed by Konstantin Stanislavsky (1863–1938) at the turn of the last century. The system is based on the belief that an actor should draw upon his or her own emotional history to become the character.

STALIN'S COLLAR

Joseph Stalin preferred his khaki military jacket to suits, so much so that in 1943, a new jacket style was designed especially for him. Featuring a sharp collar, the style was widely copied and eventually named Stalin's collar.

D

DELAUNAY,
SONIA

A cofounder of Orphism, an art movement that promoted the use of strong colors and geometric shapes, this Russian-born French painter (1885–1979) also designed textiles and stage sets. Delaunay's work is said to have influenced Elsa Schiaparelli, Jean Patou, and Guillaume Apollinaire.

B
BLINI
Smaller and more delicate than French crepes, thinner and softer than American pancakes, *blini* are a traditional Russian dish that can be eaten plain, stuffed, or with spreads such as caviar, butter, honey, or jam.

D
DUSHA

The Russian *dusha*, or soul, is a central theme of the national heritage and its composition has been explored in great depth by leading Russian minds. Sentimentality, sensitivity, and guilt are three of its defining characteristics.

M
METZENAT

Metzenat is the Russian word for "patron." Moscow's Tretyakov Gallery, one of the richest art collections in the country, was presented to the city as a gift by the textile tycoon Pavel Tretyakov in 1892. Today, the gallery houses more than 100,000 works of art. The facade was redesigned in the Russian style by the artist Viktor Vasnetsov.

МОСКОВСКАЯ ГОРОДСКАЯ ХУДОЖЕСТВЕННАЯ ГАЛЛЕРЕЯ ИМЕНИ ПАВЛА МИХАЙЛОВИЧА И СЕРГѢЯ МИХАЙЛОВИЧА ТРЕТЬЯКОВЫХЪ

ОСНОВАНА П. М. ТРЕТЬЯКОВЫМЪ ВЪ 1856 Г. и
ПЕРЕДАНА ИМЪ ВДАРЪ Г. МСКВ ВЪ 1892 И СЪ МУЗЕЮ
СЪЗАВЕЩАННЫМЪ ГОР, СОБРАНIЕМЪ С. М. ТРЕТЬЯКОВА

O
OSTAP BENDER

Dmitry Loginov, head of the successful men's fashion brand Arsenicum, dedicated a collection to the character Ostap Bender, the antihero of novels by Ilya Ilf and Evgeny Petrov. The books are satires on Soviet life centered around Bender, who calls himself "the great combiner," looks for a treasure in a chair, wears a Captain's hat, and dreams of Rio de Janeiro.

M
MEDVED

The Russian word for "bear" is *medved*, from *med* for honey and *ved* for owner. The bear, or the owner of the honey, is strong, self-assured, master of the forest and a national symbol.

K
KREMLIN

Once home to the czars, the Kremlin is a symbol of Russian political power and the official residence of the president. The first of its palaces was erected in the middle of a forest in 1156 by Yuri Dolgoruky; the historic red-brick cathedrals and towers were built between 1485 and 1495 by Renaissance architects, including Pietro Antonio Solari.

SUMMER
BEAUTY
ISSUE

LIBERMAN,
ALEXANDER

Alexander Liberman (1912–99) moved
to New York in 1941 and took a job at
Vogue. He worked for Condé Nast for
53 years as an art director and editorial
director, and was responsible for the cre-
ative development of its magazines.

30 pages about
YOUR
SUMMER BEAUTY

Beauty and Vitamins
Thirty-day Beauty Plan
Beauty in the Open

...AND MORE

· MAY 15. 1941

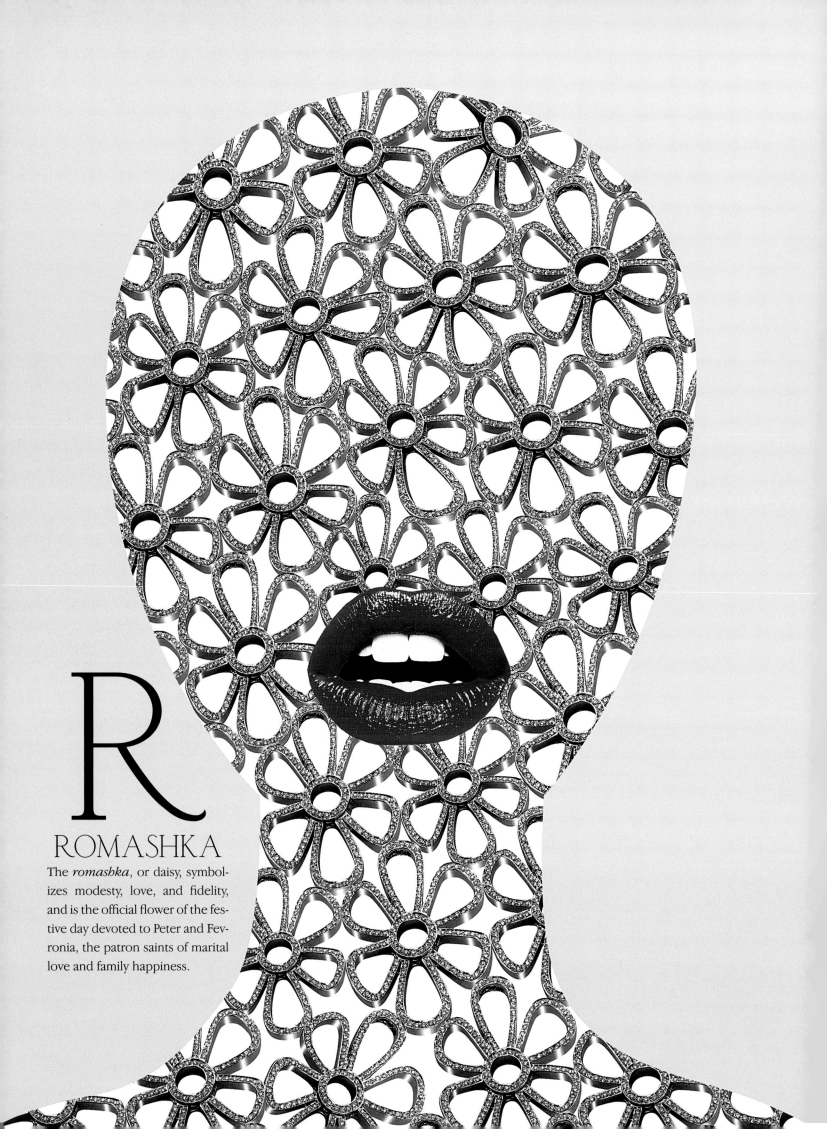

R
ROMASHKA

The *romashka*, or daisy, symbolizes modesty, love, and fidelity, and is the official flower of the festive day devoted to Peter and Fevronia, the patron saints of marital love and family happiness.

P

PELMENI

Traditionally, these meat-filled boiled dumplings were cooked in large batches and stored outside, frozen, for several months at a time. Today *pelmeni* are usually made fresh; they are often served on New Year's Eve with sour cream, vinegar, and ketchup.

K
KOSINKA

The *kosinka* is one-half of the square piece of fabric known as a *platok*. After the revolution a red *kosinka* came to symbolize a woman who worked to survive, and the style was adopted by female commissars and members of the Communist Party.

C

CASSINI, OLEG

The son of Russian count Alexander Loiewski and grandson of the Russian ambassador to the United States during the McKinley and Theodore Roosevelt administrations, Oleg Cassini (1913–2006) became a leading American fashion designer, best known for dressing Jackie Kennedy during her years as first lady.

K

KITMIR

During her exile in Paris, the Grand Duchess Maria Pavlovna (1890–1958) met her brother's lover, Coco Chanel, and worked for her as an embroiderer. Subsequently, she launched her own award-winning embroidery business in the early 1920s, called Kitmir.

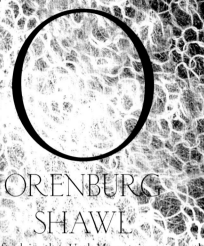

ORENBURG SHAWL

Handcrafted in the Ural Mountains since the 17th century, Orenburg shawls are made from weblike, finely knit lace in neutral colors such as white, beige, or gray—depending on the goat fiber. The shawls are so lightweight that you can easily pull one through a wedding ring. The contemporary Russian knitwear designer Ludmila Norsoyan uses this traditional technique in her collections.

B

BABA YAGA

This witchlike Slavic fairy-tale character lives in a forest hut built on chicken legs. Portrayed as an old hag with a collection of magical objects at hand, though she is believed to be wicked, she often helps the good. An unkind or not-so-beautiful woman can be referred to as a "Baba Yaga."

P

PARFIONOVA, TATIANA

Maya Plisetskaya, Natalia Vodianova, Carine Roitfeld, and Diana Vishneva are all fans of Saint Petersburg–born Tatiana Parfionova, an award-winning designer known for capturing Russian culture in her collections.

N
NAGRADA

Nagrada is the Russian word for "award," and the Russian most associated with awards is former Soviet leader Leonid Brezhnev, who received more than 100 of them in his lifetime. He was criticized for lavishing himself and his party members with honors and medals, and the Soviet system of conferring awards was changed after his death in 1982. Ironically, Brezhnev's love of medals, and his penchant for wearing so many of them at a time, inspired a fashion trend.

P

PETER THE GREAT

During the reign of Peter I (1672–1725), Russia became an empire and the czar its emperor. He instituted sweeping reforms of the church, military, and government, as well as Russian culture. Visits to the West led him to rethink tradition: He simplified the alphabet and reformed the calendar. On January 4th, 1700, a decree abolishing the traditional Russian style of dress was issued, and from then on, the nobility wore Western clothing.

M
MONOMAKH'S CAP

According to legend, this 13th-century coronation crown of gold filigree, decorated with pearls, emeralds, rubies, and fur was given to Vladimir II Monomakh, ancestor of the Russian czars, by his grandfather, the Byzantine emperor Constantine Monomachus. It is stored in the Kremlin armory.

N
NEFT

The first Russian oil refinery was founded in 1745, during the reign of Elizabeth Petrovna. Today Russia is the world's second-largest producer and exporter of oil, after Saudi Arabia.

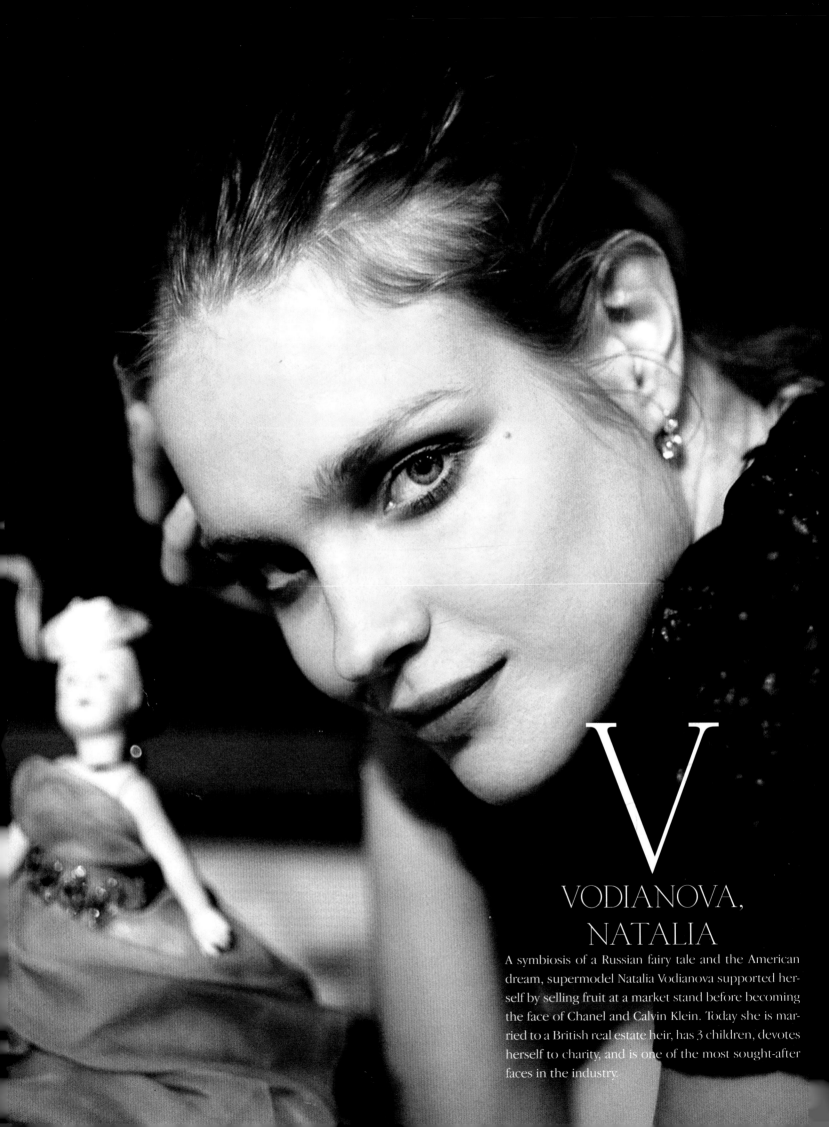

V
VODIANOVA, NATALIA

A symbiosis of a Russian fairy tale and the American dream, supermodel Natalia Vodianova supported herself by selling fruit at a market stand before becoming the face of Chanel and Calvin Klein. Today she is married to a British real estate heir, has 3 children, devotes herself to charity, and is one of the most sought-after faces in the industry.

S

SESTRA

In Russian the word *sestra* means both "sister" and "a woman help-
ing those in need." During the 19th century, women who worked in
hospitals were called "sisters of mercy" and wore uniforms that looked
very much like a nun's robe. Over time Russian nurses officially became
known as "sisters."

B
BOLSHOI THEATER

One of the most famous theaters in the world, the Bolshoi was the site of countless historic premieres, from Tchaikovsky to Rachmaninoff. The company was founded in 1776. The theater opened in 1825 and has remained a magnet for opera and ballet connoisseurs.

S

SHAHMATI

Probably the most well-known game in the world, chess or *shahmati* is a rare combination of sport, science, and art. It originated in India and China, and reached Western Europe and Russia in the early 9th century. Many Russian rulers, including Ivan the Terrible and Peter the Great, were dedicated to the checkered board. Since 1927, with few exceptions, almost all world chess champions have been Russian.

R
RUBASHKA

In 1920 Coco Chanel fell in love with Grand
Duke Dmitri Pavlovich; in 1922 she designed
the Russian Collection, transforming peasant
blouses and village clothes into the dernier cri
of Paris.

H

HOYNINGEN-HUENE, GEORGE

Baron George Hoyningen-Huene (1900–68), the son of a Baltic nobleman and military officer and the grandson of an American minister to Russia, fled to Europe with his family during the revolution and worked his way up as a fashion photographer at French *Vogue*. His sophisticated, classical style influenced his successors, including Horst, Irving Penn, and Richard Avedon.

P

PEREBOR

The Russian word for "over the top," *perebor*, can mean running one's fingers over guitar strings, but more loosely refers to exceeding reasonable limits with regard to makeup, accessories, or even diamonds.

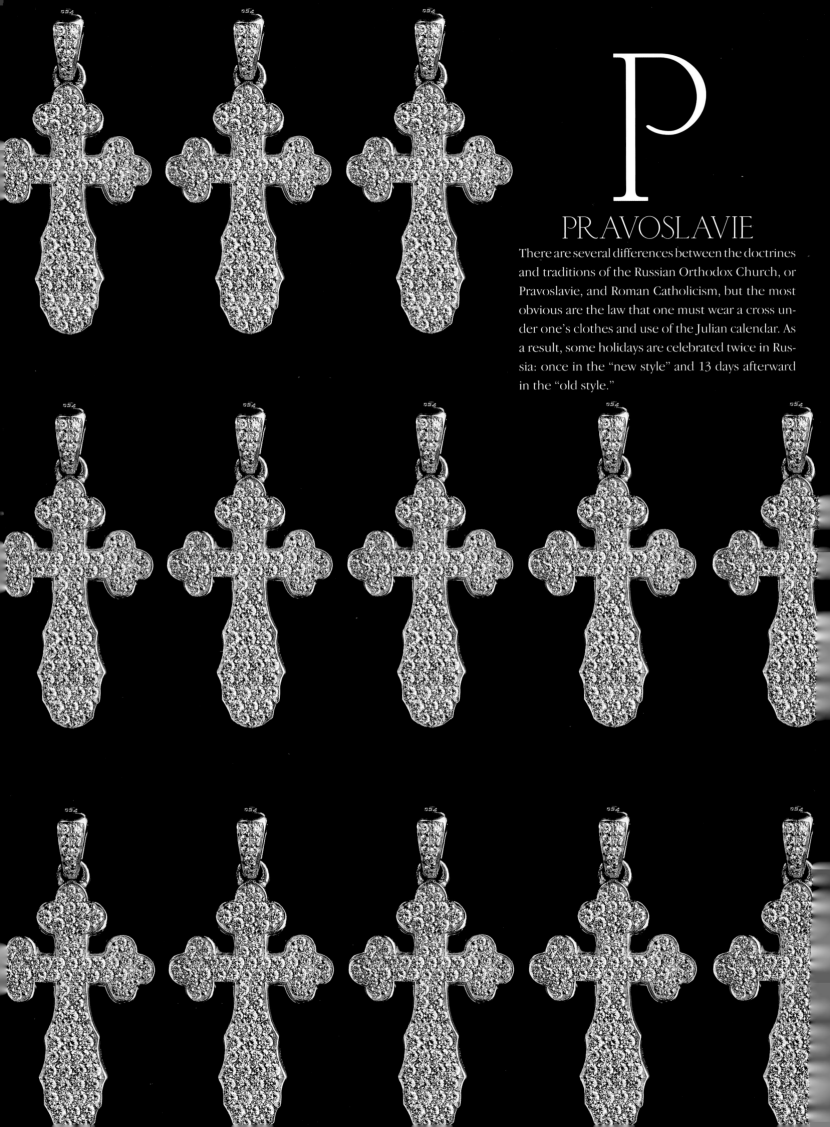

P

PRAVOSLAVIE

There are several differences between the doctrines and traditions of the Russian Orthodox Church, or Pravoslavie, and Roman Catholicism, but the most obvious are the law that one must wear a cross under one's clothes and use of the Julian calendar. As a result, some holidays are celebrated twice in Russia: once in the "new style" and 13 days afterward in the "old style."

C

CATHERINE THE GREAT

Despite Marlene Dietrich's portrayal in *The Scarlet Empress* (1934), Catherine II (1729–96) is remembered by Russians not for her numerous lovers but for her 34-year reign, during which she instituted many positive reforms, including a dress code for the royal court inspired by traditional Russian costumes, the passage of laws limiting the sovereign's will, the founding of the first boarding schools for women, and the establishment of Russia as an international power.

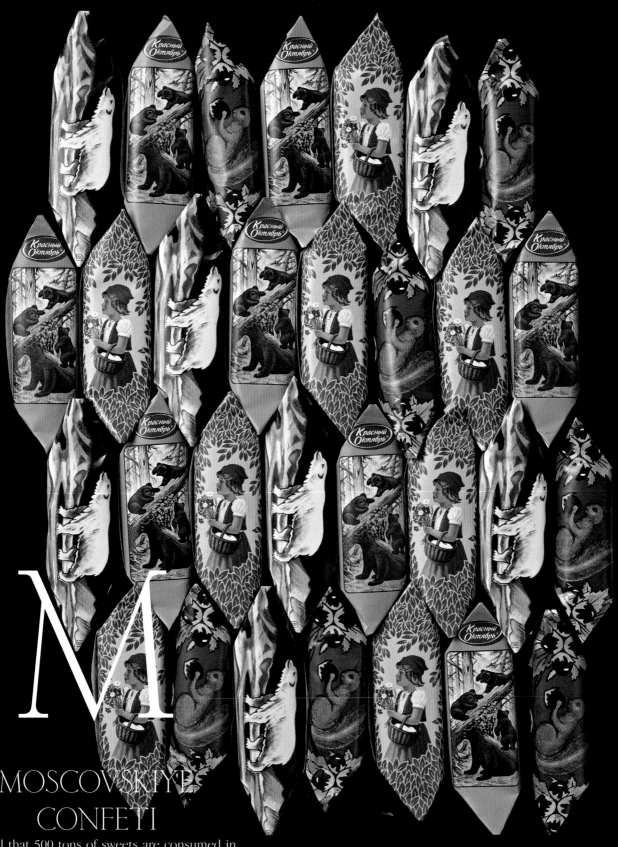

M
MOSCOVSKIYE CONFETI

It is said that 500 tons of sweets are consumed in Moscow daily. These praline-flavored waffle candies are one popular variety. Some sweets are still made according to centuries-old recipes. At the beginning of the 20th century there were more than 30 candy makers in Moscow, but only a handful survived the revolution.

B
BALALAIKA

This triangular stringed musical instrument has a mythical quality; forest ghosts were said to have helped people upon hearing its sounds. At the turn of the century, it was a part of a Russian soldier's uniform.

R
RIBALKA

Russian folklore often portrays happiness as something you have to sit and patiently wait for, just like fishing. Hence the fishing party is a Russian male-bonding ritual, an occasion when men join together and enjoy fish soup cooked over a bonfire.

B
BEREZKA

With more than 60 varieties, the birch has long been one of Russia's greatest icons. According to folklore, the white-branched birch specifically is endowed with magical powers. In the 1960s, a fashion chain called Berezka opened in Moscow and became famous for selling scarce, imported goods. Here, the artist Vladislav Manishev Monroe wears a birch costume.

S
SKIPETR, VENETZ, DERZHAVA

The orb, scepter and imperial crown were each considered attributes of the czar's power and used in coronation ceremonies. Before Peter the Great's elder brother Ivan V, all Russian czars were coronated with Monomakh's Cap. In 1721 Peter replaced the cap with the imperial crown of Russia. Today all imperial regalia are are stored at the Kremlin.

G

GASSILINE, CYRILLE

Former assistant to designer Dominique Sirop in Paris and to the fashion historian Alexander Vasiliev in Moscow, Cyrille Gassiline presented his first collection in 2007 during Russian Fashion Week, where it was met with rave reviews. He finds his inspiration in the rich past of imperial Russia, the beauty of Saint Petersburg, the Soviet avant-garde artists, and the ballets of Sergei Diaghilev.

115

P

POBEDA

Pobeda is the Russian word for victory, and while the Allied troops liberated France from the Nazis, the Soviet army pushed the Germans all the way back to Berlin and raised the victory flag over the Reichstag in 1945. Russia suffered the greatest losses in World War II—it is said that there were more than 40 million casualties. Victory Day is commemorated in Russia on May 9 each year. It is a day of remembrance and sorrow, as well as a celebration of the glory of the Russian military.

Y
YUDASHKIN, VALENTIN

Russia's most prominent brides order their wedding gowns from him, celebrities frequent his fashion house on Kutuzovsky Prospect in Moscow, and he has even designed the new Russian Army uniform. Yudashkin rose to fame in 1991 with his collection of dresses inspired by Fabergé eggs and has since become a known name in fashion.

I
IRFE

Fleeing the Bolshevik revolution, Princess Irina and Prince Felix Yusupov (Rasputin's assassin) escaped to Paris with 2 Rembrandts and founded the fashion house Irfe in 1924—an acronym of their names. The label closed in 1931 and was relaunched in 2008 by designer Olga Sorokina and Yusupov's granddaughter Xenia Sfiris.

K
KOKOSHNIK

The *kokoshnik* is a traditional women's head-dress, worn with a *sarafan*. It was a symbol of aristocracy before the reforms of Peter the Great and later worn by village women as a sign of marriage. A woman wearing a *kokoshnik* remains an icon of Russian beauty.

M
MALEVICH, KAZIMIR

Kazimir Malevich (1878–1935) founded the avant-garde Suprematist movement in 1915 and is best known for his painting *Black Square,* which he created that same year for the Futurism exhibit in Saint Petersburg (then called Petrograd). *Black Square* became a modernist icon and symbol of the new art.

R
REVOLUTION

The 1905 uprising of a crew of Russian sailors against their oppressive czarist officers on the battleship Potemkin foretold the October 1917 revolution. This famous story is dramatized in Sergey Eisenstein's *Battleship Potemkin* (1925), which is considered one of the greatest films of all time.

alenaakhmadulina   alenaakhmadulina

AKHMADULINA, ALENA

Drawing upon the decorative patterns pictured in Russian folklore and fairy tales and the vibrant illustrations of Ivan Bilibin, contemporary fashion designer Alena Akhmadulina's dresses are deeply rooted in the national culture.

M
METRO

Decorated with mosaics and stained-glass ornaments, Moscow's metro stations are true palaces underground designed by some of Russia's best architects. In addition to Moscow, six Russian cities—Saint Petersburg, Nizhniy Novgorod, Novosibirsk, Yekaterinburg, Samara, and Kazan—have metro service.

L
LENIN

One of the most influential figures in Russian history, Vladimir Lenin (1870–1924) was the leader of the Bolsheviks, the organizer of the October Revolution, a founder of the Soviet Union, and the author of more than 40 volumes of articles. His radical appearance—3-piece suits, a goatee, and a mustache—paired well with his politics.

P

PRAVDA

Pravda was the name of the Communist Party's newspaper, which was published from 1912 through the Soviet era. The word *pravda* means "truth," and there is still a Russian publication with this name.

P
PAPAKHA

Best recognized as part of the Cossack uniform, the *papakha* is a high, cylinder-shaped wool hat originally secured with a chin strap. Each Cossack regiment had its own *papakha* and a unique way of wearing it.

B

BARYSHNIKOV, MIKHAIL

One of the greatest ballet dancers of the 20th century, Baryshnikov fled the USSR in 1974 and became the principal dancer of the New York City Ballet under George Balanchine. His award-winning performances were broadcast on television, and "Misha" became the world's most-recognized dancer, a heartthrob and symbol of the charismatic Russian lover, and eventually a film star.

S

SNEG

Sneg, or "snow," is synonymous with Russia, so it's no wonder that snow-themed characters abound. Ded Moroz, the Russian Santa Claus, is followed everywhere by his granddaugher, Snegurochka, who usually is dressed in a light-blue fur coat and matching hat. Winter is said to end when Snegovik, the Russian snowman, melts.

B

BALLETS RUSSES

Sergei Diaghilev's legendary avant-garde ballet company premiered the work of dancers and choreographers such as Vaslav Nijinsky and George Balanchine, composers Igor Stravinsky and Serge Prokofiev, and featured set design and costumes by such artists as Léon Bakst and Alexander Benua in each of its sensational seasons, from 1909–29.

agrandir a 0,150 ➝

G^me SAISON RUSSE

И·А
БУНИН

4

А.С. Пушкин

В.В.
НАБОКОВ

4

Ф. М. ДОСТОЕВСКИЙ

И. С. ТУРГЕНЕВ
Дворянское гнездо

ЧЕХОВ

БОРИС
ПАСТЕРНАК

Доктор
Живаго

L
LITERATURE

Pushkin, Tolstoy, Dostoyevsky, Chekhov, Bunin, Sholokhov, Solzhenitsyn, Nabokov, and Pasternak are among the very many world-renowned Russian authors whose works explore the drama and mystery of the Russian soul.

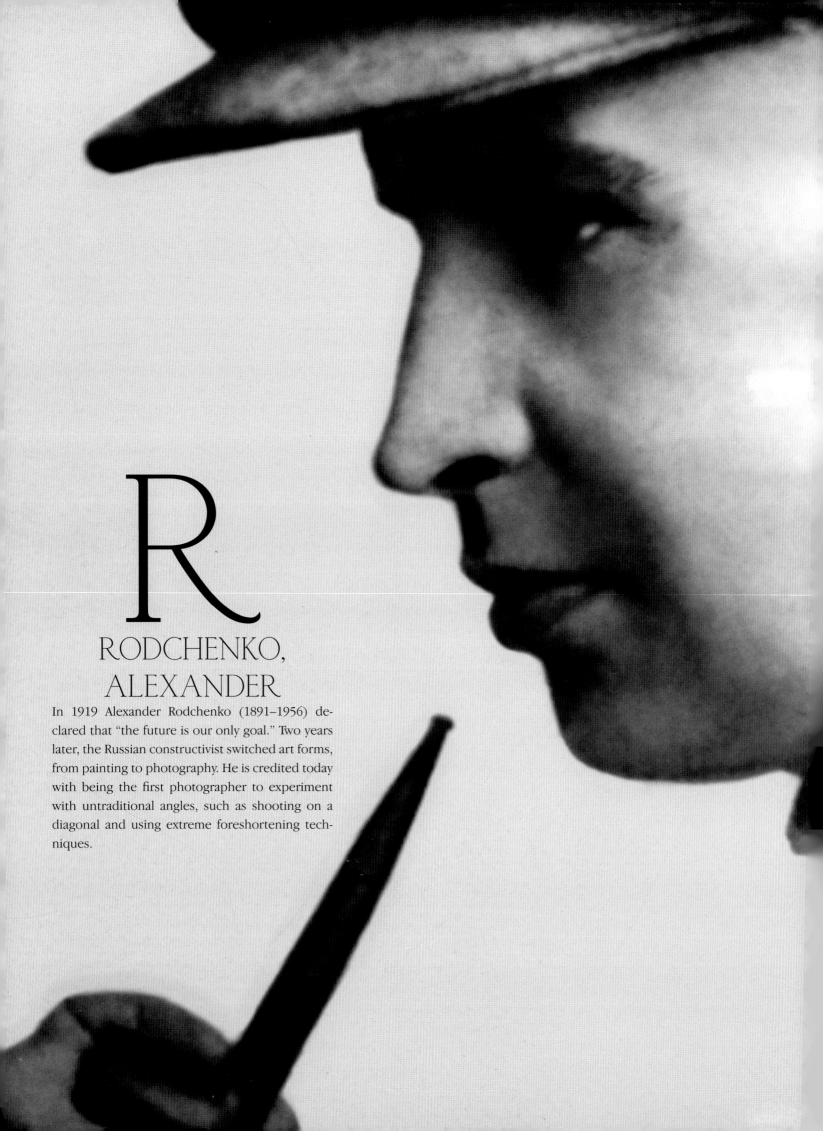

R

RODCHENKO, ALEXANDER

In 1919 Alexander Rodchenko (1891–1956) declared that "the future is our only goal." Two years later, the Russian constructivist switched art forms, from painting to photography. He is credited today with being the first photographer to experiment with untraditional angles, such as shooting on a diagonal and using extreme foreshortening techniques.

Comment a-t-on osé faire un film de LOLITA ?

L
LOLITA

"Lolita, light of my life, fire of my loins. My sin, my soul. . . ." This story of a middle-aged man's passion for a 12-year-old girl, written by Vladimir Nabokov (1899–1977), was released in English in 1955 to much controversy. Thanks to Nabokov, "Lolita" and "nymphet" have entered the international lexicon as terms for sexually precocious girls.

METRO-GOLDWYN-MAYER et SEVEN ARTS PRODUCTIONS présentent un film de JAMES B. HARRIS et STANLEY KUBRICK

LOLITA

JAMES MASON · SHELLEY WINTERS · PETER SELLERS et SUE LYON
vec   dans le rôle de "Lolita"

éalisation de STANLEY KUBRICK   Scénario de VLADIMIR NABOKOV d'après son roman "Lolita".   Production de JAMES B. HARRIS

C
CAFTAN

The first images of the caftan in Russian folk-lore appeared in 1071. Caftans were decorated with lace-embroidered silk collars and golden or bronze buttons. The main types of caftans were Turkish (long and straight, with a fastener near the neck or on the left side) and Stano-voy (detachable at the waist, with wide, often short, sleeves).

N

NU POGODI

Inspired by the Tom and Jerry stories, *Nu Pogodi*, or *Just You Wait!* is a popular cartoon series that relates the adventures of a rowdy wolf and an intelligent hare. Only 20 episodes have been created since the series' inception in 1969. "*Nu pogodi!*" has become a Russian catchphrase.

V

VOLOGODSKOYE KRUZHEVO

The root of the Russian word for "lace," or *kru-zhevo,* means "encircle" or "surround." While almost every landowner had his own serf lace makers, the capital of Russian lace became Vologda, known for its solid designs and special patterns. According to tradition, seeing lace in a dream means that one's cherished desires will come true.

Вологодское кружево

1979

к **15**

ПОЧТА
СССР

B

BRODOVITCH, ALEXEY

The legendary artistic director of *Harper's Bazaar* from 1934–58, Brodovitch shaped modern magazine design, introducing the double-page spread, turning text into a graphic object, and shifting from illustrations to photographs by rising young talents such as Irving Penn and Richard Avedon.

Made to Order Beauty

T

TSUM

This department store was founded in 1857 and originally named Muir & Mirrielees after its Scottish owners. TSUM is currently an important fashion destination in Moscow and represents more than 1,000 luxury brands, including the coolest young Russian designers.

B

BANYA

To grasp the mystery of the Russian soul and the secret to Slavic beauty, one must visit the traditional Russian spa, known for its intense steam rooms, invigorating plunges into ice water and snow, and beatings with dried birch leaves.

M

MOKEEVA, TAMARA

In the late 1970s, Tamara Mokeeva was introduced to Raisa Gorbachev. When she became first lady in 1985, Mrs. Gorbachev trusted her entire wardrobe to Mokeeva, promoting the designer's work globally and creating a vibrant and memorable image of the Russian woman.

пользоваться общественным транспортом. Тонкая, с рисунком ткань выбрана неслучайно — она более других подходит жительницам городов. Отдельные элементы костюмов и пальто (такие, как широкие проймы), возможно и выпадают из русла острой моды, но соответствуют духу времени, напряженному темпу современной жизни. Разумеется, в костюмах присутствуют черты нынешней моды: жакеты и блузы слегка приталены, линия плеч подчеркнута. Обратите внимание — некоторые признаки остромодного костюма — мини-юбка, к примеру, — в обеих моделях отсутствуют. Именно поэтому они подходят большинству женщин. Из-за разных обстоятельств далеко не все могут, да и хотят носить мини-юбку: одной помешает возраст, другой — излишняя полнота, третьей — не самая красивая форма ног. Климат — еще одно препятствие на пути триумфального шествия мини-юбки по просторам России. Тем более, что юбка «нормальной» длины или широкие брюки вполне в стиле сегодняшнего дня. Наши читатели в большинстве случаев стараются точно скопировать «ход» мысли художника, очевидно, считая, что иначе придумать невозможно. Правда, обычно так оно и бывает. Ну, а об ансамб-

В СТИ
ВРЕМЕ

V
VALENTINA

Fleeing the revolution, Valentina Nicholaevna Sanina Schlee (ca. 1894–1989) moved in 1923 to New York, where she opened her own fashion house and designed clothes and costumes for Hollywood stars including Katharine Hepburn, Gloria Swanson, and Greta Garbo. Her favorite color was black; her style was timeless.

U
USSR

The Union of Soviet Socialist Republics was a constitutionally socialist state composed of 15 republics spread across Eurasia. Founded in 1921, the USSR collapsed in 1991 as a result of Gorbachev's reforms.

C
CHEKHOVA, OLGA

The wife of a relative of Anton Chekhov, Olga Chekhova (1897–
1980) moved to Germany in 1920 and became a favorite actress of
the Third Reich. It is said that when Heinrich Himmler came to arrest
Chekhova in early 1945, he found her drinking coffee with Hitler, a
great fan. She was sent to the Soviet Union later that year but eventually returned to Berlin and lived in a home that was said to have
been paid for and guarded by the Russians.

M
MAT

A Russian patois based on the use of 4 vulgarities and curse words. The exact meaning of the word depends on the emotional mood of the author and the same words can express a great range of feelings from rage to delight. *Mat* makes it possible to have a conversation using only obscenities; speaking it in a public place is illegal.

D
DEREVNYA

While some traditional styles, such as the *sarafan* and the *paneva* disappeared from *derevnya,* or Russian villages, in the 20th century, other folkloric costumes and fabrics, especially bright floral prints and head scarves, survived and define village dress to this day.

B
BOGATYRI

These legendary heroes of folklore were strong, brave men who fought dragons and defended Russia from its enemies. The *budenovka*, a distinctive hat created by painter Viktor Vasnetsov for the Soviet Army uniform, was originally called a *bogatyrka*, after the caps worn by these mythic heroes.

M
MIKHALKOVA, TATYANA

The wife of Russian film director Nikita Mikhalkov and a former model, Tatyana Mikhalkova launched the young designers' competition "Russian Silhouette" with her charity foundation. She is the mother of three and a national style icon. Her signature look is a black turtleneck and capris worn with a bright shawl and a black velvet headband with a bow.

B
BISTRO

"Bistro! Bistro!"—"Faster! Faster!"—is what starving Cossack soldiers were said to have shouted in French taverns after their defeat of Napoleon. The word enriched the French vocabulary, and taverns became known "bistros." Russians still think they are all too slow.

M

MUZH

The Russian *muzh*, or husband, adds as much drama to the relationship as his female counterpart. Actor, singer, songwriter, and poet Vladimir Vysotsky (1938–80), one of the country's most legendary, had so many talents and such an effect on Russian culture that he was referred to as a "bard" and achieved cult status. He married the Russian-born French actress Marina Vlady in 1969 and spent the last 11 years of his life with her between France and Russia. It is said that over 1 million people attended his funeral.

P

PIONEER

Similar to the West's Boy and Girl Scouts but with a stronger political and ideological bent, membership in the Pioneer youth movement was all but compulsory for children ages 9 and older. Pins with Lenin's profile and red neckties were part of their everyday uniform, and side caps and white shirts, with blue trousers or skirts, were worn on festive occasions.

T

TEPLOV, SERGUEI

The conceptualist style of this fashion designer from Yekaterinburg captivates with a combination of cruelty and femininity. His smart and sexy dresses are for strong-willed women with perfect bodies. This dress was designed for *L'Officiel* Russia's Tricolor Exhibition.

V
VISOTKI

This group of buildings, dubbed the "7 sisters," was the USSR's response to American *visotki*, or skyscrapers. Constructed in 1947 to commemorate Moscow's 800th anniversary, these landmarks of Stalin's Empire style showcased the Soviet way of life.

L
LUBOVNITZA

Her initials are the first letters of *lubov*, the Russian word for "love." Famous for her charm, Lilya Yurievna Brik (1891–1978) was the muse and mistress of the poet Vladimir Mayakovsky, the wife of publisher and literary critic Osip Brik, and a confidante of Yves Saint Laurent. In 1978, she committed suicide. She ordered that her remains be dispersed and only a stone with 3 letters—LUB—marks her passing.

N
NUREYEV, RUDOLF

In 1961, the brilliant Russian dancer and dandy Rudolf Nureyev (1938–1993) defected at a Paris airport while under investigation by the KGB. Nureyev feared impending imprisonment and sought political asylum. For many years he petitioned the Soviet government to return to visit his mother, but his request was not granted until 1989.

M
MUKHINA, VERA

A friend of Nadezhda Lamanova, the sculptor Vera Mukhina (1889–1953) is best known for her stainless-steel monument *Worker and Kolkhoz Woman* (one figure holds a hammer, the other a sickle), which was the centerpiece of the Soviet Pavilion at the 1937 World's Fair in Paris and an iconic ideological symbol.

T
TOVARISCH

Tovarisch refers to a companion or an accomplice, but during Soviet times it came to mean "comrade"—the good citizen who shared Communist ideals. In the 1939 film *Ninotchka*, Greta Garbo plays the perfect *tovarisch*. Her character was inspired by Alexandra Kollontaï.

S
SHKOLNAYA FORMA

Both desired and detested, the Soviet school-girl's uniform, worn between 1948 and 1984, dates back to the dress style of young noble-women in the institutes created by Catherine the Great in the 18th century. The uniform consisted of a simple brown dress with a white collar and cuffs and black apron, symbolizing equality and the Soviet ideal. A Young Pioneer tie was worn around the neck, and white aprons were added on special occasions.

CZAR

From the Latin word *caesar,* "czar" was the main title of the Russian monarchs until Peter the Great declared himself emperor. Informally, "czar" was used as a royal title until Nicholas II was dethroned in 1917.

D
DIMKOVO
Another colorful Russian tradition, these brightly painted ceramic figurines—often of women in historical festive dress—are hand-crafted in the village of Dimkovo by local women.

T
TRETYAKOVSKY
PROEZD

This posh street was built in 1871 by the Tretyakov brothers, who also gave Russia the Tretyakov Gallery. The street closed during the Soviet era and was restored in early 2000. Now Tretyakovsky Proezd is the Moscow address of many international luxury brands, including Ralph Lauren, Prada, Armani, Dolce & Gabbana, Graff, and Bentley.

DACHA

Chekhov's plays turned a log house in the country used by urbanites as a weekend retreat into a national cult. Today, the *dacha*, or second home, can refer to anything from a simple hut to a multimillion-dollar mansion. During the Soviet era *dachas* were allocated according to rank. A proper Russian *dacha* should feel simultaneously homey and eclectic.

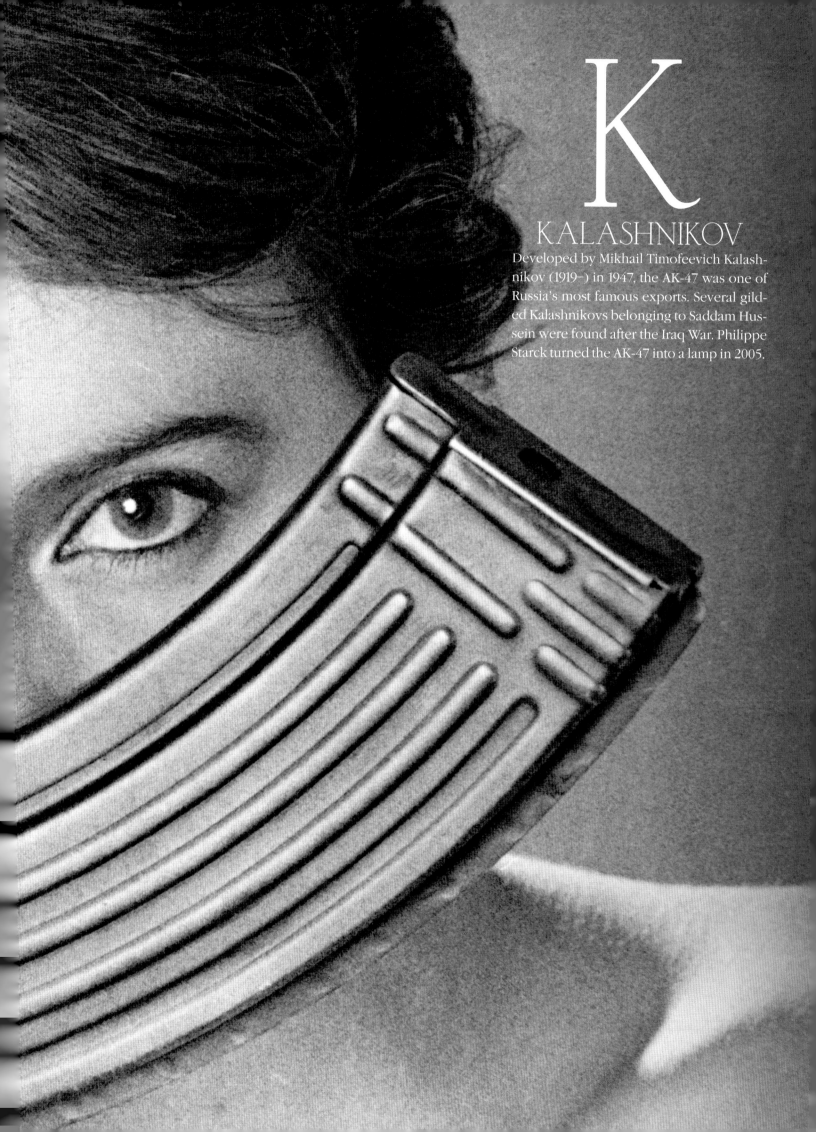

K
KALASHNIKOV

Developed by Mikhail Timofeevich Kalash-nikov (1919–) in 1947, the AK-47 was one of Russia's most famous exports. Several gild-ed Kalashnikovs belonging to Saddam Hus-sein were found after the Iraq War. Philippe Starck turned the AK-47 into a lamp in 2005.

DENIS SIMACHEV

G
GZHEL

A style of ceramics that takes its name from the small Russian village in which it was first crafted, *gzhel* originated in Russia after Peter the Great returned from Holland and reformed Russian culture. The white-and-blue motif was inspired by Dutch wares decorated in the Chinese porcelain style.

P
PARCHA

Parcha, or silk brocade, first appeared in Russian churches and courts, and it became a traditional, domestically produced fabric in the 18th and 19th centuries. *Parcha* was once prohibitively expensive and is still considered a luxury, but today it is more accessible and often featured in the collections of contemporary fashion designers.

S
SITETZ

This thin, printed cotton fabric was produced in many factories, including the famous Trehgornaya Manufaktura in Moscow. Initially a luxury item, *sitetz* became more widespread with the onset of industrial manufacturing methods in the early 19th century, thus making its bright, multicolored patterns a national staple.

212

A
ANASTASIA

Anastasia Nikolaevna Romanova was a daughter of the last czar of Russia, Nicholas II. The entire royal family was shot by the Bolsheviks in 1918, but Anastasia was said to have survived. Although the rumor was proven false, there were many pseudo-Anastasias after her death, and her legend is told in literature and film, including Anatole Litvak's 1956 movie *Anastasia*, starring Ingrid Bergman.

B

BABUSHKA

Although the word "babushka" translates as "grandmother," in the international fashion vocabulary, it refers to a head scarf tied under the chin, a look common among elderly women in the Russian countryside. The style entered Western culture in the 1950s via Jackie Kennedy and Grace Kelly.

OVSIEV, OLEG

A former accessories designer for Esprit, Oleg Ovsiev creates clothing for the Russian Viva Vox Fashion House. He is inspired by art deco and photography.

D

"DAVAI! DAVAI!"

"Do it! Do it!" is what hot-tempered Russian soccer fans shout during close matches. The first soccer game in Russia was held in Saint Petersburg in 1893, but *kila*, a game using a leather ball stuffed with horsehair, was played for centuries before that. *Footbalka* is now the Russian word for T-shirt.

K

KOSA

A traditional hair braid decorated with a satin ribbon is one of the symbols of Russian beauty. Today the best-known blond braid belongs to tennis player Anna Kournikova.

CAPTIONS & CREDITS

p. 12–13: Dmitriy Loginov, Vassa, Alexander Shumsky, Julia Dalakian, Max Chernitsov and Olga Romina standing in Red Square, Moscow for the Russian Fashion Week. Image by Vadim Gortinskiy for *Hello* Russia.
© Vadim Gortinskiy for *Hello* Russia.
p. 14: Former ELITE model Alexandra Egorova wearing a Dior haute couture dress by John Galliano inspired by constructivist paintings by artists such as El Lissitzky, Nikolay Suetin and Kazimir Malevich. Image by Fabio Chizzola. © Fabio Chizzola.
p. 15: The first cosmonaut, Yuri Gagarin, in the cockpit of the spacecraft *Vostok-1* before blastoff. © STF/RIA-Novosti.
p. 16: *Zvezda,* by artist Alexey Beliayev Guintout, 2002. © Alexey Beliayev Guintout, courtesy Triumph Gallery, Moscow.
p. 17: Models wearing clothes by Nina Donis. Image by Alexey Sedov for *L'Officiel* Russia, n°26, 2001. © Alexey Sedov.
p. 18: *Dlia Golosa* (For the Voice)*,* El Lissitzky designed this edition of thirteen poems by Mayakovsky. Conserved at the Mayakovsky Museum, Moscow. Image by Sattar Mamedov, 2008. © Sattar Mamedov.
p. 19: *Imperial Bust (Sailor)* by artist Boris Orlov, 1975. © Stella Art Foundation.
p. 20: Religious outfit decorated with *shitye* (golden embroidery). Image: "Pravoslavie" by Igor Gavrilov, 1993. © Igor Gavrilov.
p. 21: "Matrioshka" jewelry project by French designer Ora-ito for *L'Officiel* Russia, n°50, 2003. © Ora-ïto.
p. 22–23: Denis Simachëv posing for his own ad campaign with a helicopter of his own design. © Denis Simatchëv.
p. 24: Russian poet Anna Akhmatova (1889–1966). © Nappelbaum/STF/RIA-Novosti.
p. 25: Garment design by Varvara Stepanova. © Estate of Varvara Stepanova/RAO, Moscow/VAGA, New York.
p. 26–27: Ballet dancer Maya Plisetskaya in *Swan Lake* by Russian composer Piotr Tchaikovsky. Image by Evgeniy Umnov, 1960. © Evgeniy Umnov/Photosoyuz.
p. 28: Zhostovo platter. Image by Andrei Bronnikov, 2005. © Andrei Bronnikov.
p. 29: Traditional Russian *garmonika* accordion. © Russian Look.
p. 30–31: Gorky Park gate. Image by Roman Shelomentsev. © Roman Shelomentsev.
p. 32: Portrait of Alexandra Kollontaï. © ITAR-TASS.
p. 33: Popular Russian singer Alla Pugatcheva. Image by Valery Plotnikov. © Valery Plotnikov.
p. 34: Drummers marching in Red Square, Moscow, 13 September 2007. Image by Grigory Sysoyev. © Grigory Sysoyev /ITAR-TASS/Corbis.
p. 35: Black rye bread and salt, 2005. Image by Andrei Bronnikov, 2005. © Andrei Bronnikov.
p. 36–37: Chayka, Moscow, 1969. Image "Chaiki of our youth" by Viktor Akhlomov. © Viktor Akhlomov.
p. 38: Alkogolitchka T-shirt by Denis Simatchëv. © Denis Simatchëv.
p.39: "The Russian Rocket," hockey player Pavel Bure, 1990. Image by Igor Utkin. © ITAR-TASS.
p. 40–41: May Parade, 1931, Moscow. Image by Ivan Shagin. © The Moscow House of Photo.
p. 42: Tennis player Maria Sharapova celebrates at the end of her match against compatriot Elena Bovina at the Italian Masters tennis tournament in Rome, 13 May 2005. Image by Max Rossi. © Max Rossi/Reuters/Corbis
p. 43: Soviet premier Leonid Brezhnev in a suit by designer Alexander Igmand, 1981. Image by Vladimir Musaelyan. © ITAR-TASS
p. 44–45: Champion figure skater Evgeni Plushenko in Red Square. Image by Igor Vasiliadis for *L'Officiel* Russia n °72, 2005. © Igor Vassiliadis.
p. 46: Cellist Mstislav Rostropovich at the Concert for Peace in Salle Pleyel, Paris. Image by Richard Melloul. © Richard Melloul, Diego Goldberg/Sygma/Corbis
p. 47: View of Podium Concept store, Kuznetskiy Most, Moscow. © Podium.
p. 48–49: AL Models Management model Gragina wearing white fur coat. Image by Maxim Repin for *L'Officiel* Russia n°92, 2007. © Maxim Repin.
p. 50: Peasants' festive clothes, 1900s, Nizhegorodskaya province, Russia. © The State Historical museum, Russian National Library, Moscow.
p. 51: AL Models Management model Alex wearing Chapurin by Igor Chapurin and a Boucheron necklace. Image by Maxim Repin for *L'Officiel* Russia n°95, 2008. © Maxim Repin.
p. 52–53: Young Siberian girl wearing traditional clothes with reindeers, 1990. Image by Georgyi Korcheregin. © Georgyi Korcheregin/Photosoyuz.
p. 54: Russian gymnast Alina Kabaeva, world champion in 1999, performs during the rhythmic gymnastics Grand Prix in Kiev. Image by Mikhail Chernichkin. © Reuters/Corbis.
p. 55: *Chanel n°5.* Image by Didier Roy. © CHANEL/Didier Roy.
p. 56: Fashion designer Slava Zaitsev with model Lisa Virgasova-Andronova. Image by Valery Plotnikov, 1982. © Valery Plotnikov.
p. 57: *Haute coupure* by artist Dmitry Tsvetkov, idea by Mikhail Krokin, 2004. Image by Alexander Gradoboev. © Dmitry Tsvetkov, courtesy Krokin Gallery.
p. 58: Borscht graphic design with diamonds by Anton Ginzburg for *L'Officiel* Russia n°60, 2004. © Anton Ginzburg.
p. 59: Khokhloma. Image by Andrei Bronnikov, 2005. © Andrei Bronnikov.
p. 60–61: Space dogs Belka & Strelka. Image by Yuri Krivonosov, 1960. © Yuri Krivonosov/Photosoyuz.
p. 62–63: Sculpture made of *valenki* boots by artist Andrey Bartenev. Image by Eduard Basilia for *L'Officiel* Russia n°15, 2000. © Eduard Basilia.
p. 64: Actress Orlova Lubov wearing a dress by fashion designer Nadezhda Lamanova in the movie *The Circus*, by director Grigoriy Alexandrov, 1936. © All rights reserved.

p. 65: Masha Kalinina, winner of the Moscow Beauty contest in 1988, in Red Square. Image by Alexander Chuchmichev. © ITAR-TASS
p. 66: Red Stars model Polina Tasheva wearing *loskutki*-style clothes. Image by Vlad. © Vlad Loktev.
p. 67: ELITE model Valeria Avdeeva wearing a Carré scarf by Hermès, makeup by Topolino. Image by Inaki for cover of *L'Officiel* Russia n°50, 2003. © Inaki, Studio G, Paris.
p. 68: Golden samovars. Image by Vladimir Smirnov, 2004. © ITAR-TASS
p. 69: Portrait of actor and theater director Konstantin Stanislavsky, Moscow, 1935. © AFP/Getty Images.
p. 70: *Picasso-CCCP, n°34,* by artist Vagrich Bakhchanyan. © Vagrich Bakhchanyan, courtesy POP/OFF/ART GALLERY.
p. 71: View of Saint Basil's Cathedral in Red Square, Moscow. Image by Tim Graham. © Tim Graham/The Image Bank/Getty Images.
p. 72–73: Grace Models model Yulia Barbasheva wearing Roberto Cavalli, Dolce & Gabbana and Sergio Rossi in Sotchi. Image by Andrei Bronnikov for *L'Officiel* Russia, n°69, 2005. © Andrei Bronnikov.
p. 74: Portrait of artist Erté. Image by Jack Nisberg. © Jack Nisberg/Roger-Viollet.
p. 75: *Oscillante* by artist Sonia Delaunay, tapestry conserved at the Gallery La Demeure. © Keystone/Eyedea/Everett Collection.
p. 76: Blinis. Image by Dmytry Borko. © Dmytry Borko/Fotosoyuz.
p. 77: " I give you a birth, Buratino!" Artemiy Shumsky sitting in a field. Image by Artur Tagirov. © Artur Tagirov.
p. 78–79: View of the Tretyakov Gallery Museum in Moscow. Image by Roman Shelomentsev, 2007. © Roman Shelomentsev.
p. 80: Fashion designer Dmitry Loginov wearing his own design before his show. Image by Daniil Baushev, 2006. © Daniil Baushev.
p. 81: White polar bear by artist Andrey Bartenev, 2004. Image by Alena Polosuhina, 2008. © Alena Polosuhina.
p. 82: View of Kremlin *Spasskaya* tower at night with fireworks. Image by Fedor Savintsev, 2005. © ITAR-TASS.
p. 83: *Vogue* magazine cover by Alexander Liberman, May 1941. © Condé Nast Publications.
p. 84: Flower collage, by Andrey Bartenev, jewelry by Giorgio Visconti, for *L'Officiel* Russia, n°68, 2005. © Andrey Bartenev.
p. 85: Pelmeni. Image by Andrei Bronnikov, 2005. © Andrei Bronnikov.
p. 86: Red Stars model Vera Vachnadze wearing a *kosinka*. Image by Vlad Loktev for *L'Officiel* Russia n°12, 1999. © Vlad Loktev.
p. 87: Fashion illustrations by designer Oleg Cassini. © All rights reserved.
p. 88: Grand Duchess Maria Pavlovna, owner of the Kitmir dressmaking shop in Paris, 1926. © Topical Press Agency/Getty Images.
p. 89: Orenburg shawl. Image by Andrey Bronnikov, 2005. © Andrei Bronnikov.
p.90: Prestige models Ksenia Agafonova and Ekaterina Semenova and Persona model in the forest. Image by Mikhail Korolev for *L'Officiel* Russia n°32, 2001. © Mikhail Korolev.
p. 91: Ludwig Reiter boot embroidered by fashion designer Tatiana Parfionova. © Tatiana Parfionova.
p. 92: "Chanel" project by artist Dmitriy Tsvetkov. Image by Alexander Gradoboev, 2006.. © Dmitriy Tsvetkov, courtesy Krokin Gallery.
p. 93: Peter the Great Medallion. © All rights reserved.
p. 94: Shapka Monomakha. © Kremlin Museum.
p. 95: *$* sculpture by Andrei Molodkin, 2007. © Andrei Molodkin, courtesy Orel Art Gallery.
p. 96: Natalia Vodianova with Armani doll at a fundraiser for her children's charity, Naked Heart Foundation. Image by Frederic Aranda, 2007. © Rex USA/Everett Collection.
p. 97: *Farfor.* Image by Andrei Bronnikov, 2005. © Andrei Bronnikov.
p. 98: Portrait of Rasputin, early 20th century. © Hulton-Deutsch Collection/Corbis.
p. 99: *Nun 3* by artist Oleg Dou. © Oleg Dou, courtesy Aidan Gallery.
p. 100–101: View of the Bolshoi theater. Image by Anatolyi Goryinov, 2005. © Anatolyi Goryinov/Fotosoyuz.
p. 102: *Putin (Pictures of Caviar),* by artist Vik Muniz, 2008. © Vik Muniz/Licensed by VAGA, New York, NY.
p. 103: Chess set from the permanent collection of the San Francisco Museum of Modern Art. Image by Anton Ginzburg. © Anton Ginzburg.
p. 104: *Complex premonition (Man with yellow shirt)*, oil on canvas, 1928–1932, by Kazimir Malevich. © Russian State Museum, St. Petersburg, Russia
p. 105: Two men wearing bathing suits climbing toward two models wearing jersey bathing suits designed by Lucien Lelong, ca. 1929. Image by George Hoyningen-Huene. © Condé Nast Archive/Corbis.
p. 106–107: Moscow's Millionaires' Salon. Image by Dmitry Kostyukov, 2007. © Dmitry Kostyukov/AFP.
p. 108: Jewelry by Alena Gorchakova. © Alena Gorchakova
p. 109: Marlene Dietrich in *The Scarlet Empress,* 1934. © Everett Collection.
p. 110: Moscow candy. Image by Andrei Bronnikov, 2005. © Andrei Bronnikov.
p. 111: A Russian balalaika with four strings, ca. 1950. © Hulton Archive/Getty Images.
p. 112: Man fishing in the countryside. Image by Igor Gavrilov, 1977. © Igor Gavrilov.
p. 113: Artist Vladislav Mamyshev-Monroe wearing a birch costume. Image by Alexander Lepeshkin, 2003. © Alexander Lepeshkin.
p. 114: Russian crowns, scepter, and orb. Image by Nikolai Rakhmanov. © Nikolai Rakhmanov/Russian Look.

p. 115: Model Tatiana Chetaikina wearing dress by fashion designer Cyrille Gassiline. image by Andrey Vasiliev for Cyrille Gassiline © Cyrille Gassiline.

p. 116–117: Victory banner flutters over Berlin Reichstag. Image by Yevgeny Khaldei, May 1945. © ITAR-TASS.

p. 118: Black Model Management model Vanya wearing new Russian army uniform by fashion designer Valentin Yudashkin. Image by Slava Philippov for *GQ* Russia. © Slava Philippov.

p. 119: Princess Irina Youssupov wearing coat by Irfe and tiara by Chaumet. © Collection Chaumet Paris.

p. 120: *The Swan Princess* by artist Mikhail Vrubel. © Tretyakov Gallery, Moscow.

p. 121: *Black Square,* oil on canvas, by Kazimir Malevich, ca. 1923 from the Russian State Museum, Saint Petersburg, Russia. © Scala/Art Resource, NY.

p. 122–123: Image from the movie *Battleship Potemkin,* by director Sergei Eisenstein. © All rights reserved.

p. 124: Invitation card to Alena Akhmadulina's fashion show, 2006. © Alena Akhmadulina.

p. 125: Moscow metro. Image by Ruslan Krivobok, 2006. © STF/RIA-Novosti.

p. 126: *Red Lenin* by Andy Warhol, 1968. © Andy Warhol Foundation/Corbis.

p. 127: "Pravda" plate by Fornasetti. © Fornasetti. www.fornasetti.com.

p. 128: Actress Geraldine Chaplin wearing a *papakha* in the movie *Doctor Zhivago* by director David Lean, 1965. © All rights reserved.

p. 129: Russian dancer Mikhail Baryshnikov in Saint Petersburg. Image by Valery Plotnikov. © Valery Plotnikov.

p. 130–131: *Snegoviki* project by artist Nikolai Polissky, 2006. © Nikolai Polissky.

p. 132: Model wearing gypsy-style clothes and holding guitar, image by Sergei Voronin. © Sergei Voronin/Photosoyuz.

p. 133: Drawing from the *Opéra et Ballet Russes* fall/winter 2005–06 collection by fashion designer Yves Saint Laurent. © Fondation Pierre Bergé–Yves Saint Laurent.

p. 134: Palekh badge. Image by Andrei Bronnikov, 2005. © Andrei Bronnikov.

p. 135: Cover *L'Officiel* Paris, n°627, 1976. © Les Editions Jalou.

p. 136: President Agency model Olga Ius wearing jewelry. Image by Roman Morozov. © Roman Morozov.

p. 137: Onion dome ring by Alena Gorchakova. © Alena Gorchakova.

p. 138: Raisa and Mikhail Gorbachev. Image by Wojtek Laski. © Wojtek Laski/Eastnews.

p. 139: Background of Y's fashion show with Soviet army choir. Image by Marcio Madeira. © Marcio Madeira/Firstview.

p. 140–141: The Amber Room, Catherine Palace, Saint Petersburg. Image by Sergei Velychkin, 2003. © STF/RIA-Novosti.

p. 142: Costume sketch by artist Léon Bakst for a Bacchante, from the ballet *Narcissus,* 1911. Image by Erich Lessing. © Erich Lessing/Art Resource, New York.

p. 143: Dancer Vazlav Nijinsky from Sergei Diaghilev's Ballets Russes. © All rights reserved.

p. 144–145: Great Russian authors' books. Image by Alla Polosuhina, 2008. © Alla Polosuhina.

p. 146: Artist Alexander Rodchenko holding a pipe. © RIA-Novosti.

p. 147: Poster for the movie Lolita directed by Stanly Kubrik, 1962 © *Swim Ink 2, LLC/Corbis.*

p. 148: *Prince Ivan and the Firebird,* illustration by artist Ivan Bilibin for the Russian fairy-tale *The Firebird,* published in Saint Petersburg, 1901. © The Bridgeman Art Library.

p. 149: "Nu Pogodi" jewelry by Denis Simatchëv. © Denis Simatchëv.

p. 150–151: Stamp. Image by Andrei Bronnikov, 2005. © Andrei Bronnikov.

p. 152: *Harper's Bazaar* cover. Image by Ernest Beadle, graphic design by Alexey Brodovich, October 1946. © *Harper's Bazaar,* New York.

p. 153: Facade of TSUM department store. © TSUM.

p. 154–155: Women in public baths. Image by Sergei Voronin, 1998. © Sergei Voronin/Photosoyuz.

p. 156: Models wearing clothes by fashion designer Tamara Mokeeva from *Journal Mod.* © All rights reserved.

p. 157: Fashion designer Valentina sitting on a cushion wearing a long sleeve black dress of her own design, ca. 1940. © Condé Nast Archive/Corbis.

p. 158–159: Fountain *Druzhba Narodov,* U.S.S.R. monument, Moscow. Image by Sergei Borisov, 2005. © Sergei Borisov.

p. 160: Actress Olga Tchekhova. © Content Mine International/Alamy.

p. 161: *Nenormativnaya jivopis* by artist Avdey Ter-Oganyan, 2002. © Avdey Ter-Oganyan, courtesy M&J Guelman Gallery.

p. 162–163: Young village girls wearing old women's clothes. Image by Evgeniy Umnov, 1958. © Evgeniy Umnov/Photosoyuz.

p. 164: *Tri bogatirya* by Aglaya Feneva. Image by Sergei Borisov, 2005. © Sergei Borisov/Aglaya Feneva.

p. 165: Tatyana Mikhalkova. Image by Vladimir Shirokov for *L'Officiel* Russia n°50, 2003. © Vladimir Shirokov.

p. 166: Waiter walking on terrace of café, Paris, France. Image by Bruno De Hogues. © Bruno De Hogues/Stone/Getty Images.

p. 167: Designer and socialite Dasha Zhukova. Image by Viktor Boïko. © Viktor Boïko (www.vitorboyko.com).

p. 168: *Lapti* shoes. Image by Andrei Bronnikov, 2005. © Andrei Bronnikov.

p. 169: Shapka. Image by Andrei Bronnikov for *L'Officiel* Russia, n°50, 2003. © Andrei Bronnikov.

p. 170: Surrealist painter Salvador Dalí and his wife Gala, 1940. © EFE/Corbis.

p. 171: Actor-singer Vladimir Vysotsky with actress and wife Marina Vlady. © RIA-Novosti.

p. 172–173: Young pioneer from Artek pioneer camp. Image by Igor Gavrilov, 1968. © Igor Gavrilov.

p. 174: Fashion designer Serguei Teplov and Grace Models model Irina Gorban wearing dress by Serguei Teplov. Image by Aleksey Kolpakov for *L'Officiel* Russia n°95, March 2008. © Aleksey Kolpakov/Serguei Teplov.

p. 175: Model wearing Soviet flag as a dress with *Ukrania Hotel* in the background. Image by Sergei Borisov, 1987. © Sergei Borisov.

p. 176–177: Lilya Brik posing in tutu. From Valery Plotnikov's private collection. © All rights reserved.

p. 178: Dancer Rudolf Nureyev, 1977. © Sunset Boulevard/Corbis.

p. 179: Princess Natalia Pavlovna Paley, French-born fashion icon, socialite, and film actress, photographed for the French magazine *Vu,* 1933. © Rue des Archives/The Granger Collection.

p. 180: Portrait of Feodor Shaliapin by artist Boris Mihajlovic Kustodiev, 1922. © State Russian Museum, Saint Petersburg/Bridgeman Art Library.

p. 181: A small glass of vodka. Image by Andrei Bronnikov, 2005. © Andrei Bronnikov.

p. 182: Model wearing clothes by fashion designer Vika Gazinskaya, fall/winter 2007–2008 collection. Image by Aleksey Kolpakov. © Aleksey Kolpakov/Vika Gazinskaya.

p. 183: *Rabochi & Kolkhoznitza* monument by artist Vera Mukhina, Moscow. Image by Sergei Borisov, 1985. © Sergei Borisov.

p. 184: Swedish-born American actress Greta Garbo in the title role of *Ninotchka,* directed by Ernst Lubitsch, 1939. © Rue des Archives/The Granger Collection.

p. 185: Young girls wearing school uniforms. Image by Evgeniy Umnov, ca. 1950. © Evgeniy Umnov/Fotosoyuz.

p. 186: Czar Nicolas II on the train to Crimea. © Collection Cyrille Boulay.

p. 187: Cat in a tree with jewelry. Image by Roman Morozov for *L'Officiel* Russia n°48, 2003. © Roman Morozov.

p. 188–189: View of GUM department store in Red Square, Moscow. © GUM.

p. 190. Yves Saint Laurent's 2002 New Year's card featuring his dog Moujik. © Fondation Pierre Bergé–Yves Saint Laurent.

p. 191: Dimkovo dolls. Image by Evgeniy Umnov. © Evganiy Umnov/Photosoyuz.

p. 192–193: View of Tretiakovsky proezd. Image by Artur Tagirov for *L'Officiel* Russia n°50, 2003. © Artur Tagirov.

p. 194: *Vladimirskaya* icon painting by artist Bozhei Materi. © All rights reserved.

p. 195: The Fabergé "Lillies of the Valley" egg from the Forbes Collection. Image by Stan Honda, 2004. © AFP/Getty Images.

p. 196: *Toy Story* project by Oleg Dou, 2008. © Oleg Dou, courtesy Aidan Gallery.

p. 197: "Iron Wedding" Art by Anya Zholud. © Anya Zholud, courtesy Aidan Gallery.

p. 198: Model wearing *sapogi* boots from *L'Officiel* Paris n°473, 1961. © Les Editions Jalou.

p. 199: Pavlovsky Posad shawl. Image by Andrei Bronnikov, 2005. © Andrei Bronnikov.

p. 200: Greta Garbo in a portrait for *Anna Karenina,* 1935. © Everett Collection.

p. 201: IMG model Gemma Ward wearing a *pirozhok* at Prada fashion show fall/winter 2005–06. Image by Marcio Madeira. © Marcio Madeira/Firstview.

p. 202: View of Palace Square and Alexander Column, Saint Petersburg. Image by Michael Dunning. © Michael Dunning/Getty Images.

p. 203: Russian film director Andrei Konchalovsky with daughter Maria. Image by Mikhail Korolev. © Mikhail Korolev.

p. 204: *Roman Abramovich,* encaustic on canvas, by artist Jose Maria Cano, 2005. © Jose Maria Cano, courtesy Regina Gallery.

p. 205: A Russian passport. Image by Alena Polosuhina, 2008. © Alena Polosuhina.

p. 206: Russian writer Leo Tolstoy dressed in a peasant style. Image by Michael Nicholson, ca. 1910. © Michael Nicholson/Corbis.

p. 207: A traditional Russian *dacha.* Image by Roman Shelomentsev for *L'Officiel* Russia, n°68, 2005. © Roman Shelomentsev.

p. 208–209: A girl with a Kalashnikov rifle. Image by Sergei Borisov, 1985. © Sergei Borisov.

p. 210: Bottle warmer by Denis Simachëv. Image by Andrei Bronnikov, 2005. © Andrei Bronnikov.

p. 211: Model wearing a *parcha* coat from *L'Officiel* Paris, n°579, 1970. © Les Editions Jalou.

p. 212: Ivanovo printed textiles, 1983. © Khudozhnik, RSFSR.

p. 213: Actress Ingrid Bergman in the film *Anastasia,* 1956. © Bettmann/Corbis.

p. 214: Chocolate *Alenka.* Image by Andrei Bronnikov, 2005. © Andrei Bronnikov.

p. 215: Model wearing clothes by fashion designer Oleg Ovsiyev for VIVA VOX, Image by Nataly Arefieva for VIVA VOX © VIVA VOX.

p. 216: Girl in *futbolka,* painting by artist Alexander Samohvalov, 1932 © Russian State Museum, Saint Petersburg, Russia.

p. 217: Russian tennis player Anna Kournikova wearing a *kosa* braid. © Duomo/Corbis.

ACKNOWLEDGEMENTS

The author expresses her warmest thanks: *L'Officiel* which raised my plank—it is an honor to be part of our family, Prosper and Martine Assouline for their miraculous proposal to create this book which I got 5 years ago, and for making this dream a reality this year, my family who supported me through the years, Evgeniy Zmievetz (ZAO Parlan Publishing) who invited me to become *L'Officiel* Russia's editor in chief 10 years ago, Marie-Jose Jalou-Susskind (Les Editions Jalou) who was the best example for me for 10 years, Gladys Perint Palmer for introducing me to the Assouline's, the Assouline team for their patience, Aidan Salahova, Natasha Zinger, Raisa Kirsanova, Lidiya Orlova, Albina Nazimova, the late Andrey Razbash, Anton Ginzburg, Tatiana Shestopalova, Yuriy Kondratuk, Vas Sloutchevsky, Anush Gasparyan, Anna Lebsak, Vadim Dimov, Dmitriy Semakov, Igor Tchekulaev and others for their consulting and advice—smart and precious in project creation. The team: Esther Kremer,Yann Popper, Miriam Hiersteiner, Maria Ryaboff , Cyrene Mary, Michelle Mounts, Mathilde Dupuy d'Angeac, Sarah Hanson, Valérie Tougard, Perrine Scherrer, Nastya Merkulova, Seraphima Chebotar, Erika Imberti, Kristin Henn, Lew Quzmic Baltiysky, Juliya Ilyutovich. The photographers: Andrey Bronnikov, Sergey Borisov, Alena Polosuhina, Sattar Mamedov, Vadim Gortinsky for *Hello* Russia, Fabio Chizzola, Alexey Sedov, Igor Gavrilov, Roman Shelomentsev, Valeriy Plotnikov, Viktor Ahlomov, Igor Vasiliadis, Maxim Repin, Eduard Basilia, Vlad Loktev, Inaki, Artur Tagirov, Daniil Bayushev, Mikhail Korolev, Roman Morozov, Alexey Kolpakov, Alexander Lepeshkin, Vladimir Shirokov, Viktor Boyko, Wojciech Laski. The artists: Andrey Bartenev, Anton Ginzburg, Alexey Belyaev-Gintout, Boris Orlov, Ora-ïto, Dmitriy Tzvetkov, Vagrich Bakhchanyan, Vladislav Mamyshev-Monroe, Andrey Molodkin, Oleg Dou, Nikolai Polissky, Sergey Bratkov, Avdey Ter Oganyan, Aglaya Feneva, Anya Zholud, Topolino. The galleries and museums: Zelfira Tregulova/ Kremlin Museums, Alexander Borovskiy/ Risskiy Museum, Emelyan Zakharov/ Triumph Gallery, Ekaterina Finogenova/ Moscow House of Photography, Mikhail Krokin/ Krokin Gallery, Aidan Salahova/ Aidan Gallery, Sergey Popov, Alla Khudina/ Gallery POP/OFF/ ART, Ilona Orel/ Orel Art Gallery, Vladimir Ovcharenko/ Regina Gallery, Anna Svergun/ Stella Art Foundation. The stylists: Andrey Artyomov, Galina Smirnskaya, Nikitos, Jennifer Eimer, Elena Ivanova-Tagirova, Polina, Elena Bakanova, Anna Beck, Oxana Gurieva. The Fashion designers: Slava Zaitsev, Valentin Yudashkin, Denis Simachev, Tatiana Parfionova Vika Gazinskaya, Alena Ahmadulina, Cyrille Gassiline, Oleg Ovsiyev, Dmitriy Loginov, Vassa, Julia Dalakian, Max Chernitsov, Olga Romina, Nina Donis. The brands: Alice Macparbo, Nathalie Ifrah / *L'Officiel* Paris, Olga Yudkis/ Bosco di Ciliegi, Polina Kitzenko/ Podium, Alena Gorchakova, Oksana Kalinina / Alena Gorchakova, Vika Petrova/ Tsum. The heroes: Mikhail Gorbachev, Maya Plisetskaya, Alina Kabaeva, Maria Sharapova,Evgeni Pluschenko, Dasha Zhukova, Alla Pugatcheva, Pavel Bure, Masha Kalinina, Natalia Vodianova, Tatyana Mikhalkova, Marina Vladi, Andrey and Masha Konchalovsky, Alexander Shumsky/ Russian Fashion Week. The Models: Alexandra Egorova, Valeria Avdeeva/ Elite, Polina Tasheva, Vera Vachnadze/ Red Stars,Yulia Barbasheva/ Grace Models, Artemiy Shumsky, Ksenia Agafonova, Ekaterina Semenova/ Prestige, Yulia Sybbotina/ Persona model, Olga Ius/ President, Alex, Gragina / AL Model Management, Gemma Ward/ IMG.

The publisher wishes to thank: Kelly Killoren Bensimon, Euphrosine Gorvitz Adocidés, Serge Lutens, Patrice Lerat-Nagel, Lu Alexis Chasleries, Malick Kane (Getty Images), Bruno Pouchin (Roger-Viollet), Chaumet, Yuki Tintori (Fornasetti), Kim Tishle (VAGA), Marissa Caputo (IMG), Sabine Killinger (ELITE), Merrideth Miller (Condé Nast), Dilcia Johnson (CORBIS), Anna Carpentie (Ora-ïto), Bryan Walsh.